I0425301

Girls Smoking

Illustrated

By Heljä Gustafsson

Smoking and Girls: A Deadly Mix

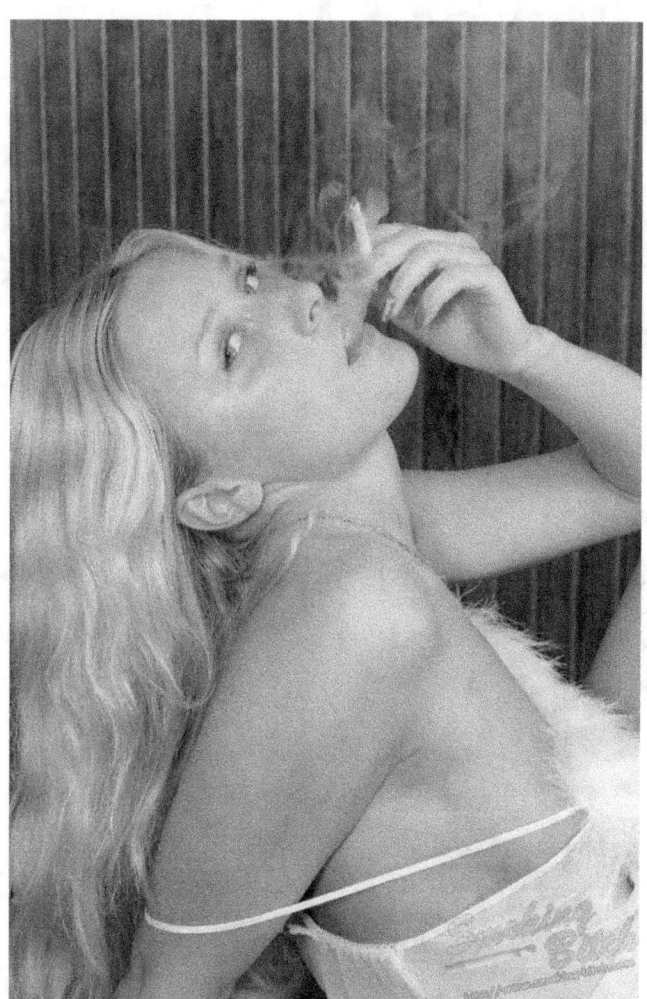

When we think of the dangers facing children today, most adults think of violence, drugs, drunk driving, teen pregnancy, and AIDS. We know that smoking is unhealthy, but most kids will try it, and many adults don't take it seriously. A new Surgeon General's report entitled *Women and Smoking*, reminds us that there has been a 600% increase in women's death rates from lung cancer since 1950, and that those deaths are a direct result of a smoking addiction that starts in childhood.

Smoking is a habit that almost always begins in youth -- usually before age 16. If a child graduates from high school without ever smoking regularly, he or she will probably never will. We think of smoking as an equal-opportunity bad habit, but the theme of the report is that smoking is a woman's issue. This theme has not yet been embraced by most women's organizations or advocates for girls or women -- but the research is persuasive. Girls are more easily addicted to nicotine than boys, and female smokers are more likely to die of lung cancer than males who smoke the same number of cigarettes. And a great deal of advertising is aimed at persuading girls that smoking is sexy, fun, and a way to show their independence.

Girls are as likely to smoke as boys, and the decreases in smoking from the 1970's to the early 1990's were reversed a few years later. For example, 40 percent of girls smoked in 1977, and this decreased to 26 percent in 1992, and went back up 35 percent just five years later (1997). However, smoking went down to 30 percent in 2000.

The results for young children also resemble a roller coaster: 13 percent of 8th grade girls smoked in 1991, compared to 21 percent in 1996, and then back down to 15 percent in 2000. Smoking rates are higher for 10th graders, but the trend is similar (21 percent in 1991, 31 percent in 1997, 24 percent in 2000).

The report points out the racial discrepancies; for example, for high school senior girls, smoking is most common among the American Indians and Alaskan Natives (39 percent), and whites (33 percent), and lowest among Hispanics (19 percent), Asian (14 percent) and African Americans (9 percent). The greatest reduction in smoking has been among black girls: only 7 percent were smoking in 1992 compared to 38 percent in 1977, and then up to 12 percent in 1998. Smoking among white girls decreased less and then returned to earlier levels -- from 40 percent to 31 percent in 1992, and then back up to 41 percent in 1998.

Girls who smoke are more likely to have parents or friends who smoke; they tend to have weaker attachments to parents and family and stronger attachments to peers and friends. They tend to take risks and to be rebellious, are less committed to school or religion, and are more likely to believe that smoking can control weight and negative moods. They also have a positive image of smokers, which can come from advertising, celebrities, or other role models. This positive image may overcome any concerns about the health risks.

Smoking continues into the young adult years, and those numbers are also rebounding: 37 percent of 18-24 year or olds smoked in 1965-6, compared to 25 percent in 1997-8; recent trends suggest the numbers are increasing again.

Smokers may make the choice to start smoking, but not everyone who dies from smoking is a smoker. Second-hand smoke can cause death from lung cancer and heart disease among lifetime nonsmokers. Infants born to smoking mothers or to mothers exposed to second-hand smoke are at increased risk of small birth weight and other developmental problems.

The statistics in the report are somewhat overwhelming, and also a bit confusing -- the trends are going down again, so why make such a fuss now? The reason, the Surgeon General reminds us, is that smoking is the cause of more than 165,000 preventable deaths among women every year. The report is an important reminder that smoking -- the most common drug addiction in the U.S. -- starts as an innocent experiment among youth, and becomes a potentially lethal habit that is very difficult to overcome. If adults tolerate it or shrug it off, they contribute to kids' perceptions that smoking is cool or at least acceptable, and not really dangerous.

Women and Smoking: A Report of the Surgeon General
April 2001

SMOKING IS A WOMEN'S HEALTH ISSUE

Since everyone already knows that smoking causes lung cancer and heart disease, what's new about women and smoking?

What you may not know is that women, regardless of their age, can be harmed by smoking – smoking contributes to infertility, anxiety, blindness and osteoporosis, to name just a few of the many health consequences. Women who smoke during pregnancy not only endanger themselves, but their babies. Mothers who smoke around their children also put their kids' health at risk.

The good news is that it's never too late to join the ever-increasing ranks of healthy nonsmokers.

This issue brief will help you better understand why smoking is particularly bad for women, how women have been persuaded to smoke, and, if you or someone you care about smoke, help you find resources to quit.

The Beginning: Girls and Smoking

Smoking is a habit that almost always begins in youth -- usually before age 16. If a teen graduates from high school without ever smoking regularly, he or she probably never will.

Over the last 30 years, the percentage of teens that smoke has decreased, increased, and then decreased again. For example, 40% of high school senior girls were current smokers in 1977, decreasing to 26% in 1992, increasing to 35% in 1997, and then decreasing to 21% in 2002.

The bad news is that while boys and girls are equally likely to start smoking, the health implications for girls and women are worse. Symptoms of addiction can appear in young people within days or weeks after smoking first begins, well before daily smoking has started. The Surgeon General's 2001 Report on Women and Smoking concludes that young women ages 18 to 24 were more likely than young men to report that they experienced symptoms of nicotine dependence.

Targeting Girls and Women

While girls and boys today have roughly equal chances of becoming smokers, this "equality" is a fairly recent phenomenon, and it didn't happen by chance. At the start of the 20th century, female smokers were rare. Smoking was equated with poor character, low social status, and prostitution. In fact, the stigma of women smoking was so great that that Congress considered banning women from smoking in the District of Columbia in 1921.

In 1928, George Washington Hill, president of American Tobacco, said that persuading women to smoke "will be like opening a new gold mine in our front yard." American Tobacco targeted women with its "Instead of a sweet, reach for a smoke" advertising campaign. It worked. Rates of female smokers soared.

The introduction of "women's cigarettes" in the late 1960s and early 1970s coincided with sharp increases in the number of girls aged 12-17 who began smoking, according to the Surgeon General's report. Virginia Slims successfully capitalized on the burgeoning women's movement with its slogan "You've come a long way, baby." Between 1967 and 1973, smoking rates more than doubled among 12-year-old girls.

Cigarette marketers target girls in several ways. In addition to depicting women smokers as beautiful, independent and fun, cigarette ads continue to send the subliminal message that smoking helps a girl keep her weight down, just as it did in the 1920s. Marketing cigarettes as "slims" or "thins" subtly reminds girls and women that smoking will help control weight. One study found that girls who dieted more than once per week were four times as likely to become smokers.

Although cigarette ads are prohibited in children's or teen magazines, billions of dollars are spent on ads in *TV Guide, Rolling Stone, Sports Illustrated*, and many other magazines that are widely read by children and teenagers. For example, one survey found that cigarette companies advertise heavily in magazines with large youth readerships, such as *People* magazine. Though technically aimed at adults, 35% of *People's* readers are teens.

Women and Smoking

Today, 21% of adult women in the U.S. smoke, compared to 26% of men -- but this gender difference is closing. Women's health shows the results. Since 1987, lung cancer has surpassed breast cancer as the leading cause of cancer deaths among women in the United States. Smoking is directly responsible for 87% of all lung cancer cases in America each year.

Smoking causes heart disease – the #1 killer of women in the U.S. Smoking causes or contributes to chronic respiratory diseases such as emphysema and chronic bronchitis, and many kinds of cancer. It also increases the chances of stroke, blindness, early menopause, osteoporosis and infertility.

Smoking affects how you look and feel

Smoking also can harm a woman's appearance and mental health. Smokers have more facial wrinkles, gum disease, dental decay, and halitosis (bad breath). The Surgeon General's Report concluded that smokers are more likely to be depressed than nonsmokers, and that women with anxiety disorders are more likely to smoke.

Do women smoke because they are anxious or does smoking increase anxiety? Many smokers believe that smoking is relaxing, but recent research indicates that smoking tends to increase a young woman's stress level rather than reducing it. One reason is that smoking can impair respiration, which can contribute to panic attacks. Nicotine itself increases feelings of anxiety, but can trick the smoker into believing that smoking is relaxing. In fact, addiction to nicotine causes stress, which is then alleviated by smoking. Although anxiety temporarily increases when an individual stops smoking, a few weeks later her anxiety level will be lower than it was when she was smoking.

Smoking and Pregnancy

Sadly, many women continue to smoke during pregnancy, despite known, widely publicized hazards to both the smoker and the fetus. The best estimates available indicate that between 12 -20% of pregnant women and girls smoke cigarettes. The carbon monoxide from tobacco use can reduce the amount of oxygen for the developing fetus and nicotine can reduce blood flow to the uterus. Pregnant women who smoke are more likely to experience life-threatening complications of pregnancy, such as a pregnancy that implants in the fallopian tube instead of the uterus, and premature labor. The Surgeon General's Report on Women and Smoking concludes that 10% of all infant deaths during pregnancy are linked to smoking. Pregnant women who smoke also increase the risk to their fetus for stillbirth, low birth weight, premature birth, and sudden infant death syndrome (SIDS).

WOMEN'S AND GIRLS' ORGANIZATIONS AND SMOKING
The increased attention to the special risks of smoking for women has resulted in a number of projects that focus on supporting tobacco cessation efforts specifically for women. Many of these efforts are being conducted by women's organizations, some of whom had not focused on this issue in the past. Here are a few noteworthy examples:

- The **National Women's Law Center** released a study in September of 2003 *Women and Smoking: A National and State-by-State Report Card*, the first comprehensive assessment of women's smoking-related health conditions and the policies that are proven to help reduce smoking among women and girls. The study grades and ranks each state and the nation on women's health status, and evaluates the strength of state tobacco control policies. The study found that most states and the nation overall fall far short of the nation's goals for reducing smoking among women and girls. In addition, neither the states nor the federal government have adopted strong tobacco control policies to help them meet these goals. They conclude that, "Stronger federal policies that regulate tobacco, promote cessation, monitor Internet sales, and fund research and data collection, among others, are critical to the reduction of tobacco use among women and girls." The report can be viewed on their website at www.nwlc.org.

- The **Mautner Project** is a national lesbian health organization, which focuses on lesbians with cancer and their caregivers. Its mission is to improve the health and well-being of women who partner with women and their families through direct services, research, education and advocacy. They work on smoking cessation throughout their programs, which include a smoking cessation support group in Washington, DC and participation in local advocacy efforts to limit smoking in restaurants and bars in Washington, DC. To learn more visit their website at www.mautnerproject.org.

- The **National Organization for Women** created a public education campaign to raise awareness and take action against tobacco advertising. The Redefining Liberation campaign was funded by a grant from the Centers for Disease Control and Prevention. During the first phase of the campaign, the NOW Foundation and the California NOW chapter created the "Redefining Liberation" video. The NOW Foundation distributed the video to NOW chapters and community organizations across the country who are using it to educate and activate people around these issues, especially young women and girls. In the second phase of the campaign, the NOW Foundation is focusing on the development of new and expanded educational materials and increased outreach. To get more information on the campaign go to www.nowfoundation.org/issues/health/whp/

- The **National Center for Policy Research (CPR) for Women & Families** conducts the Women and Smoking Public Education Project to engage women's organizations in efforts to reduce smoking among women and girls. The goals of the project are to impact women's and girls' attitudes towards smoking as well as their tobacco-related behaviors. CPR seeks to educate women and their families about how smoking is especially harmful to girls and women, in an effort to prevent tobacco addiction in the next generation of girls. The project seeks to reach over 2000 women through work with a dozen women's and girls' organizations. For more information go to www.center4policy.org

- The **Girl Scouts** (www.girlscouts.org) organization prevents smoking initiation among girls through its curriculum. Offerings include *In the Zone: Living Drug Free*, which encourages girls to learn about the negative effects of tobacco use. This project, offered in partnership with the Office of National Drug Control Policy, educates girls and teens who want to live drug-free about the realities of tobacco and other addictive drugs. *In the Zone* books offer younger girls the "real deal" on tobacco. They let tweens and teens know it isn't cool to smoke or take drugs and suggest positive alternatives.

Girls smoking

Smoking during pregnancy

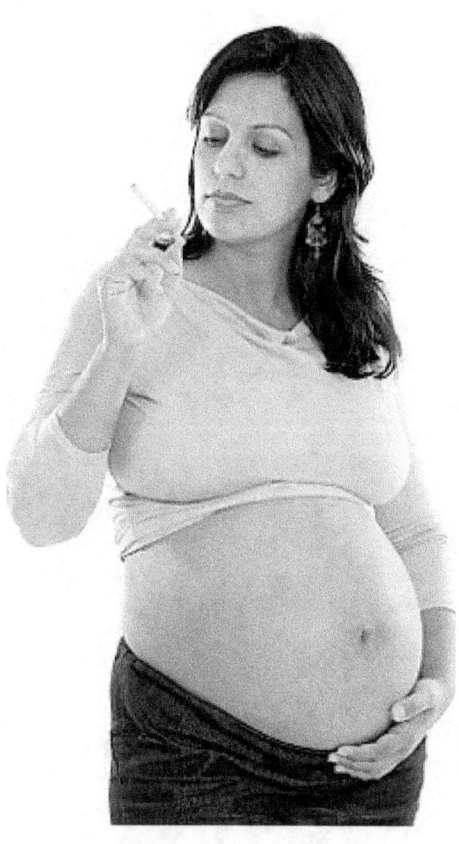

A new study conducted by British researchers revealed that pregnant women who quit smoking habit not only perk up their health, but also increase the chances of giving birth to an easygoing baby.

The study results published in the Journal of Epidemiology and Community Health believes that babies of women, who did not give up smoking habit during pregnancy, were notably annoyed and irritable.

The scientists at Britain's York University viewed more than 18,000 babies born between 2000 and 2002 as well as their mothers.

Depending upon the smoking status, the mothers were divided into four different groups, which were named as non-smokers during pregnancy, quitters, light smokers or heavy smokers (10 or more cigarettes per day).

The natures of the women's babies were evaluated when they were nine months old. The study researchers used a familiar method designed to pick up on positive mood, openness to new things and normal sleeping and eating habits in babies.

The study discovered that women who quit smoking while their pregnancy had the most easy going infants as compared with the non-smokers and the smokers. In actual fact, their children had the lowest chances of irregular behavior and of getting upset while facing new situations or things.

The study also established that heavy or chain smokers had the most difficult children.

They also noted that giving up smoking during pregnancy is linked with an urge to protect the baby, rather than any intention to quit in the long run.

"Relapse rates are high after the birth. But it indicates the capacity to adapt to different circumstances and the ability to plan and to delay gratification, characteristics which seem to be missing in those who carry on smoking", the researchers said.

The chemicals in cigarettes are harmful for the development of the brains of babies in the womb. Tobacco can affect the growth of a fetus and are also associated to low birth weight, birth defects and increased risk of cot death.

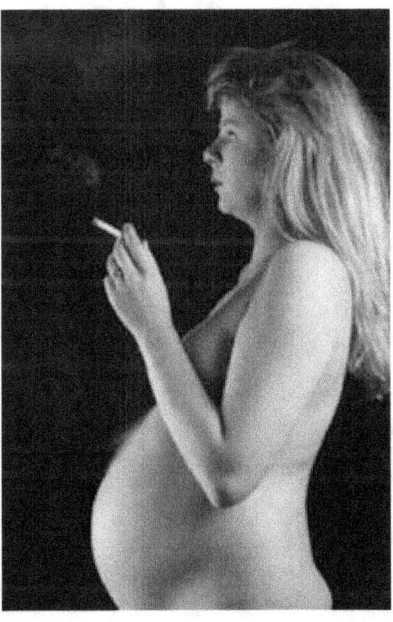

Smoking during pregnancy harms both the mother and her developing fetus. Aside from increased morbidity and mortality from cancers, cardiovascular and pulmonary disease in the mother, smoking has been implicated in the etiology of abruptio placenta, placenta previa, spontaneous abortion, premature delivery, and stillbirth.

Prenatal smoking is thought to account for about 18% of cases of low birth weight (<2500 g), and also increases risk of shortened gestation, respiratory distress syndrome, and sudden infant death syndrome. Cigarette smoking is the principal cause of low birth weight in

developed countries. Intrauterine growth retardation is the most
Cigarette smoking is the principal cause oflow birth weight in
developed countriesstrongly documented adverse effect of smoking
during pregnancy.

This is a significant public health concern because low birth weight is
the most important single determinant of neonatal and infant
morbidity and mortality. Retarded fetal growth in the offspring of
smokers may be attributable to several factors, including the
vasoconstricting properties of nicotine, elevated fetal
carboxyhemoglobin and catecholamine levels, fetal tissue hypoxia,
reduced delivery of nutritional elements and elevation of heart rate
and blood pressure.

Even after controlling for alcohol use, socioeconomic status, maternal
height, maternal weight and years of education, smoking has been
implicated in long-term effects such as poor cognitive performance on
achievement tests and decreased physical growth.

Girls smoking

Psychological effects from nicotine

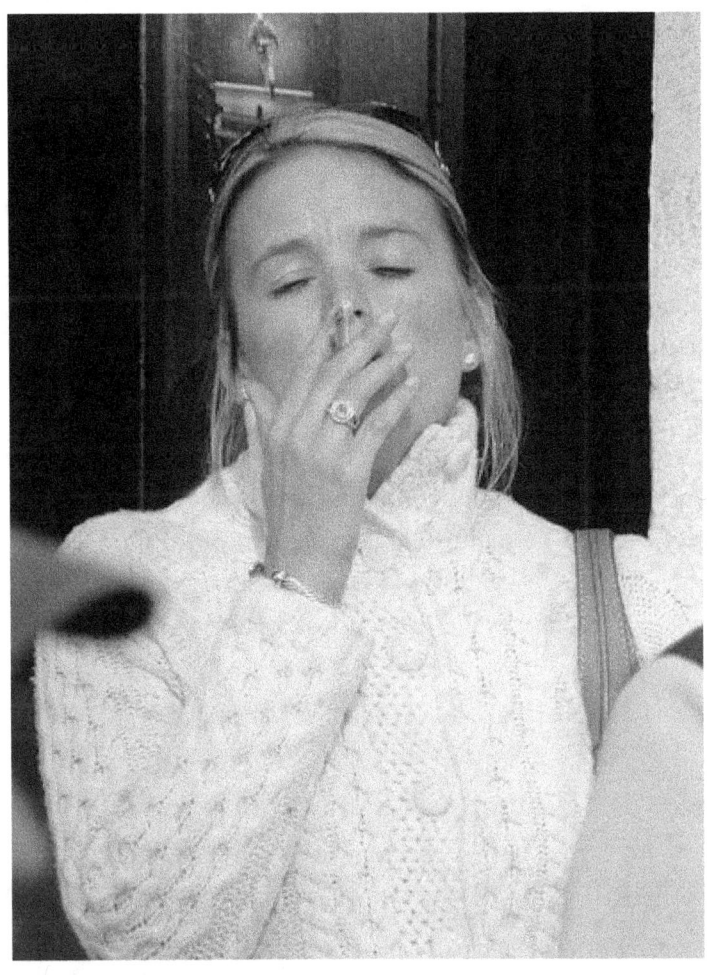

Most smokers begin at adolescence or early adulthood. The biggest reasons that young people start smoking is peer pressure from their friends. And the fact that they feel cool for doing so because they are rebelling and taking risks. The reason it is so hard for parents, schools, and doctors to inform kids that it is harmful and they shouldn't do it is because young people tend to listen to their peers before they will listen to adults. Many adolescents often feel that smoking cigarettes is the first step out of childhood and being closer to adulthood.

During the process of smoking the inhaled smoke triggers chemical reactions in nerve endings. The nicotine has chemical similarities that the natural occurring substance in your body called Acetylcholine. That is why nicotine triggers the nerve receptors as well. These receptors are part of two major neurotransmissions, these are called synaptic transmission, and paracrine signalling. These increase heart rate, memory, alertness, and gives people a slightly higher response time. Dopamine and after that Endorphins are released and that is what gives the buzzed feeling. During the early stages of smoking, like when people first start they get pleasurable feelings and sensations because of the effect of nicotine and the dopamine systems in our bodies. But as people smoke longer it takes more and more nicotine to get the same effect on their bodies. Once people have smoked for many years they often don't even get that sensation anymore and the only reason they still smoke is because the don't want to go through the withdrawal symptoms associated with trying to stop smoking cigarettes.

When you talk to people about smoking they often try to justify it and play it off as not a big deal. They often say that everyone dies sometime so smoking cigarettes isn't going to change anything. Another thing that people often say is that smoking cigarettes relieves stress or have other benefits that don't make the risks sound so bad. Many people also use the excuses that it helps them relax and other factors that make them feel justified for smoking. The fact that nicotine helps people relax is a big misconception. Studies have shown that nicotine provides stimulants and also depressant effects, and that the effect of the cigarette is determined by the mental state of the person at the time of smoking.

While tobacco companies have been forced to spend millions by courts on anti-smoking advertising campaigns, they have been furtively increasing the nicotine content of cigarettes to keep smokers addicted. According to a study by the Massachusetts Department of Public Health, nicotine in the average cigarette has gone up 10% since 1998. Experts warn that cigarettes with high nicotine content are the easiest to become addicted to and the hardest to stop using.

Girls smoking

Smoking and breast cancer

Researchers compared smoking history and other breast cancer risk factors among 1,225 women who developed breast cancer and 6,872 who did not during the first year after their initial visit to the Mayo Clinic Breast Clinic.

NEW YORK - Women taking the next puff of a cigarette might consider this: smoking 100 or more cigarettes may substantially increase their odds of developing breast cancer, researchers report.

Previous studies linked regular exercise, limiting alcohol intake, and avoiding postmenopausal obesity as lifestyle changes that can reduce women's odds of developing breast cancer, notes Dr. Ivana T. Croghan and colleagues in The Breast Journal.

The current study provides new evidence that "a woman smoker can reduce her risk of breast cancer by stopping smoking as soon as possible," Croghan commented to Reuters Health via email.

Croghan's group compared smoking history and other breast cancer risk factors among 1,225 women who developed breast cancer and 6,872 who did not during the first year after their initial visit to the Mayo Clinic Breast Clinic.

Surveys completed during this visit indicated just over 10 percent were current smokers, almost 9 percent were former smokers, and 81 percent had never smoked, Croghan, with the Mayo Clinic Nicotine Research Program in Rochester, Minnesota, and associates report.

In addition to the link with smoking, women who had used oral contraceptives for 11 years or longer had a whopping 200 percent increase in the odds of developing breast cancer. Women who used postmenopausal hormone therapy showed 81 percent increased odds, while aging raised the odds of developing breast cancer by 2 percent per year.

On the flip side, Croghan and colleagues report that having a hysterectomy decreased women's odds by 35 percent. Also, they did not see a compounding increase in risk for breast cancer among women with more than one risk factor.

Croghan noted that prior investigations with contradictory results regarding smoking and breast cancer risk did not consistently define smoking as current, former or never. The current study defines anyone who ever smoked more than 100 cigarettes at any time as having a history of smoking. Those who smoked less were considered never-smokers.

Croghan's group suggests further investigations using similar smoking definitions to assess how pre- and post-menopausal duration of smoking, amount smoked, and exposures to second-hand smoke might alter a woman's odds of developing breast cancer.

SOURCE: The Breast Journal, September/October 2009

Although smoking cigarettes has been linked to a variety of chronic health problems — including heart disease, stroke and several types of cancer — health experts have found no relationship between a woman's status as a smoker and her breast cancer risk. Over the past 40 years, dozens of studies, large and small, have found no indication that smoking cigarettes either increases or decreases the likelihood of a woman developing breast cancer.

Why this is the case is not clear. When researchers look at the relationship between smoking and other cancers, the results are dramatic: Smoking has been highly correlated to lung cancer risk, for example. Cigarettes contain many known carcinogens, and the chemical byproducts of smoking have been found in breast tissue and breast milk. So why is there no apparent connection with breast cancer?

Researchers theorize that smoking might equally increase and decrease risk because smoking acts against the production of estrogen, a hormone that plays a leading role in breast cancer. Women who smoke also are less likely to have endometrial cancer, which is related to estrogen, and tend to start menopause earlier. In theory, the anti-estrogenic effects of smoking could counter the cancer-causing effects of some of the chemicals in cigarettes.

The Surgeon General's Report in 2006 on exposure to secondhand smoke acknowledged that there is no evidence that smoking or secondhand smoke cause breast cancer but emphasized that women should not smoke because of all the other cancers and negative health outcomes that have been linked to smoking.

Despite the overall lack of data connecting smoking behavior and breast cancer, there are some small groups of women for whom cigarette smoking or exposure to secondhand smoke might increase breast cancer risk:

- Women who started smoking in their teens and who have smoked for more than 20 years might be at increased risk for breast cancer when compared with women who have smoked less than 100 cigarettes in their lifetime, according to data from the Erie County Smoking Study, reported in the January/February 2002 issue of *Chemical Health and Safety*. Though a handful of studies have supported this conclusion, other studies using data from large populations have not found an increased risk of breast cancer among lifetime smokers when compared with nonsmokers.

- Nonsmoking women who married young (before age 17) to men who smoked have an increased risk of a breast cancer diagnosis.

- Women who smoke and whose immediate female relatives have had three or more diagnoses of breast cancer or ovarian cancer among them are at increased risk for a breast cancer diagnosis.

How Smoking Affects Treatment

Another area of concern for researchers is whether being a smoker means that a woman will have a more aggressive type of breast cancer or be limited in her treatment options because of the impact of smoking on her overall health. According to a recent study of 6,000 breast cancer patients, smoking has no effect on the type of cancer or on treatment. The research results were presented to the American Society for Therapeutic Radiation and Oncology in October 2007.

SOURCES: "Cigarette Smoking Increases Risk for Cancer in High-Risk Breast Cancer Families," April 2001, *Cancer Epidemiology Biomarkers and Prevention*; "Can Active Smoking Cause Breast Cancer?" January/February 2002 *Chemical Health and Safety*; "The Health Consequences of Involuntary Exposure to Tobacco Smoke: A Report of the Surgeon General," June 27, 2006, Office of the Surgeon General, U.S. Department of Health and Human Services; "Smoking Does Not Worsen Breast Cancer," Oct 29, 2007, HealthDay News; American Cancer Society (www.cancer.org)

Girls smoking

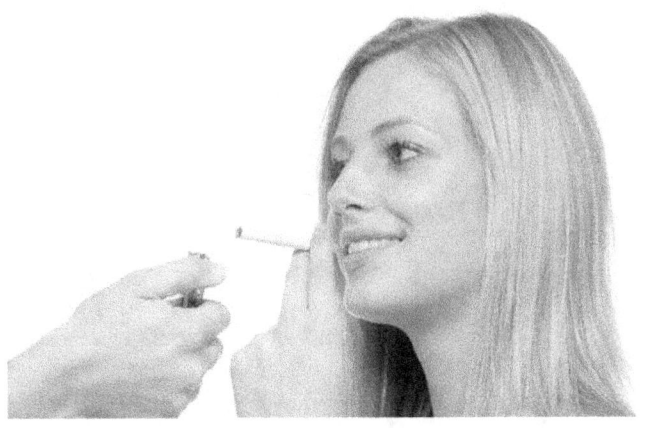

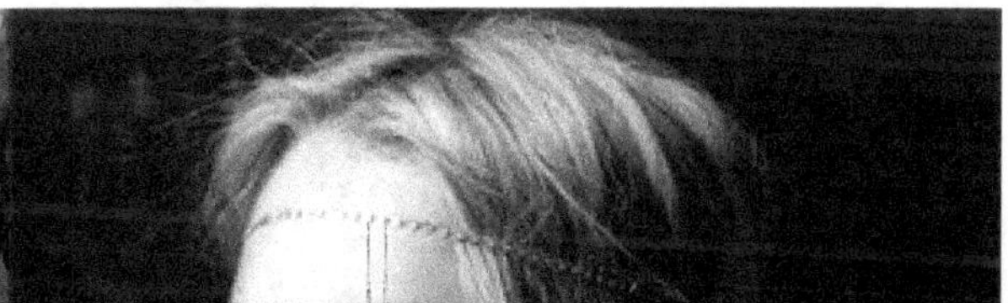

  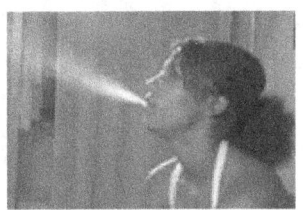

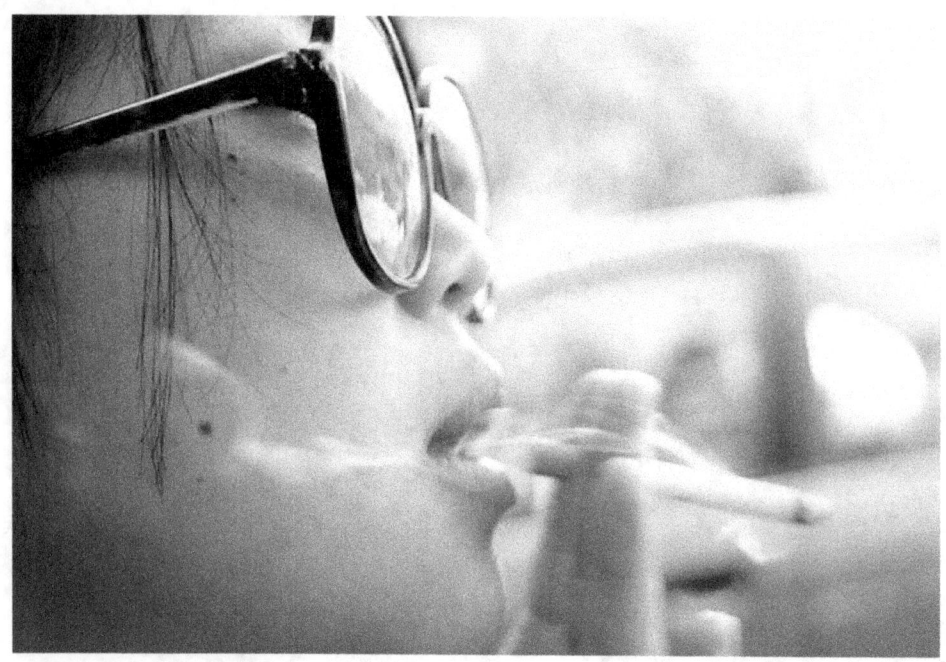

Smoking advertisement

Las Autoridades Sanitarias advierten que el tabaco
perjudica seriamente la salud.
Nic.: 1,1 mg., 0,8 mg. Alq.: 15 mg., 10 mg.

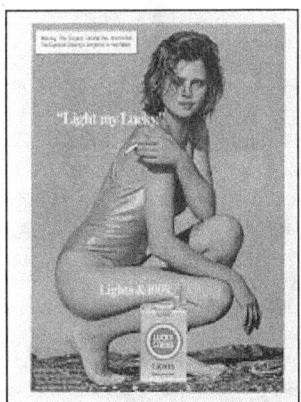

SMOKING SIDE EFFECT

Premature aging

Stillborn Child

Secondhand Smoker

Hair loss from Chemotherapy

Face Tumor

Sunken Face

Bald from chemotherapy

Burn Victim

Tracheotomy

Severe Gingivitis

Lung Cancer

Collapsed lung